THE NERVOUS FILAMENTS

Also by David Dodd Lee

Abrupt Rural
Arrow Pointing North
Wilderness
Downsides of Fish Culture

As Editor

SHADE 2004 & 2006
The Other Life: The Selected Poems of Herbert Scott

THE NERVOUS FILAMENTS

DAVID DODD LEE

Four Way Books
Tribeca

Please direct all inquiries to:
Editorial Office
Four Way Books
POB 535, Village Station
New York, NY 10014
www.fourwaybooks.com

Library of Congress Cataloging-in-Publication Data

Lee, David Dodd.
The nervous filaments : poems / David Dodd Lee.
p. cm.
Includes bibliographical references.
ISBN 978-1-884800-05-4 (pbk. : alk. paper)
I. Title.
PS3562.E3383N47 2010
811'.54--dc22
2009029459

This book is manufactured in the United States of America and printed on acid-free paper.

Four Way Books is a not-for-profit literary press. We are grateful for the assistance we receive from individual donors, public arts agencies, and private foundations.

This publication is made possible with public funds from the National Endowment for the Arts and from the New York State Council on the Arts, a state agency.

Distributed by University Press of New England
One Court Street, Lebanon, NH 03766

We are a proud member of the Council of Literary Magazines and Presses.

National Endowment for the Arts
A great nation deserves great art

State of the Arts
NYSCA

[clmp]

TABLE OF CONTENTS:

3. *To Hold in Such High Regard*

The wind is part of the process
The rain is part of the process

Pound, *Pisan Cantos*

I. THE OTHER WATER

LOVELESS, THE GRAVEL

Here is your
story, in my

horizonless competence,

a nevertheless fine
kettle of

mockingbirds

I could see ambulance spelled
backwards

I could see the eels spilling
out of the horse's head

a crawdad sits in a cold
pool importantly praying

(cumulus nimbus)

and here is your
story

coming from a different direction

a couple of shaved ideas

GEOLOGY OF THE LAKE SUPERIOR BASIN

It's such a long way down

elegance in the depth of every compulsion

although I could live
without the graffiti

all those Mastodons and the blood math . . .

and you know each meal
has a magnitude of casualness

followed by the "splitting"

but nobody admits this

the lack of punctuation will continue
the absence of church bells

the icicles grow dark as the library closes

in room after room the books disappear . . .

I have this candle and what she left on it

her smell

the economic facts—

somebody dousing a cigarette

a shirt fresh out of the cellophane

love is a form of gambling

PORCELAIN

The doors keep
accumulating

address: wouldn't you like to know . . .

just drive north

we're sad in our own country

WOLF SPIDER

It was raining inside
that picture on the wall

and the single tree
had a brown side backing a red
lacquer of trembling

leaves

an exodus

a consciousness quick on its legs

so it was with these stabs
of things seen through the wakefulness in this other boy

his vertebrae tingling

the frame emitting pure static

(inside it a freight
train shook all the milkweeds)

the briers so bad even her socks were bloody

stuck in the neck on a thorn in that single tree

I did check the bedroom

now the windows were open

WHO BUT I, O RECKLESS DEATH

It's a secret,
the blackness . . .

swimming at the heart of it

Skull open
like a pool in Beverly Hills

the way the antibiotics travel

(she wears no greatcoat)

love flung outward

the geese half-mated with swans

the blood on their wings

and so it is with the sand and the speckled eggs

two boats
two boys

trees film over with ice in the middle of summer

her hair keeps flying out of her open mouth

an owl dies on its branch

another Monday on the ring of Saturn

BORN LATE

A block of soap
carved to look like Pan

and that's just what came in the mail

a volcano under those flip flops

kisses spilling off the water-wheel

Green becomes a stillness leftover in the late-born effluence
of a decade's worth of smoke and flat beer

(I can't get any air)

because there was no acoustic guitar

just dust scraped off an anxious moth's wings

A COUNTY ROAD

A circle goes around a branch

it's a mirror of grief's ecosystem

one rhythm, two feet . . .

a duplicate radiance the water implies
because it's watching too

green herons in a panic under the raceway nets

the largest sturgeon emerges
and spits a fine pile of shells into a basket of roots

pastoral as purgatory

head not heavenly with clouds

feet swinging above terra firma

And the day before yesterday?

Everything nothing

she finally stepped off the heavy table and waited

tunnel sinking and then rising under the Detroit River

all of her sisters singing together with their eyes squinting shut

no hidden agenda

no discussion the next morning

ROMANTIC

You
and the weather inside you

the graham crackers the blue jay flips and eats

a certain lack of love

after all that's your head in the window

looking out

through rain
through snow

lonely lonely

One of the new jobs we have is dating

you work in reality TV—

the myth of the soul mate

The new staircase covered with sub-prime money

then carpet (chiropractor green)

is part of it . . .

couples holding hands with silk over their nude bodies streaming
past stars during Ascension . . .

Erase it all remember the scotch pine, the shovel under the streetlight

driving with Kim

the way the flakes dimpled
the surface of our cups of hot chocolate

They shredded the moon again she said about the falling snow

THE PYRAMIDS

You were born with a moral sense

which is why the dry colored leaves
swirling in autumn
bring tears

one by one they burdened the enormous blocks
closer and closer to heaven

a wick of blood for your name

you can see it in the bubbles in this rum and Coke

I only felt a peculiar sense it was something
like an island, the *Cape*

the softest murdering
reason has invented

the way the arm breaks off

buried in the ocean floor

the sound of money
reproducing itself
in a vault under carpet in the northwestern-most

bathroom

They have a floor but no eyes

you boil them alive

who wouldn't have a nervous breakdown

RETRIBUTION

There was a hinge—

the door swung one way

creaking

you could see buses
out near the quad

men with bags and bayonets . . .

or was it your night-light

a man on his naked back laughing into her failed cornfield of a face

don't call me an idiot

the suburbs

jail for Irish farmers

he had a key

a searchlight in his pants

it swung back the other way

THE SEVENTIES

Singly, right from birth frankly,

I'd find the shadow

That was leaning like a tree
Away from my father.

The cherry blossoms shook in the Massachusetts . . .

A bit of the pilgrim
In it

Polished wood floors

Sunshine and the sexuality of chocolate

First, there was the business
With the lawyers,

And the rolling boat of my bed,

The room bright in deep water

For the waving of the lobster claws.

I moved with the clouds,

Pencils turned into cigarettes.

And then she's under you,
Smelling of sheetrock, stained by antibiotics,

Half-naked,

Crying on the apple-moss.

THE OTHER WATER

Lake with the invisible coast

and the February fog

it's true she had trouble breathing

you stack your social
skills on top

multiplication tables in your daydreams

like sleeping in an oxygen tent . . .

I was the one

everyone wanted her taste on their fingers

that smell of exhaust in your hair

joint after joint

Connie on the greenest moss

she died
they die

Caves where you go to live
houses on fire

the boat

she didn't want me to see her under a certain light

2. AUTOMATIC THANK-YOU KISSES

I AM NEVER GOING BACK

Come in. Listen to the wind
express itself.

Inveigle a dying dream.

I like my antelope feminine—
marinated in a closet . . .

But I came necessary to masturbation
like a key deer.

It's what the oceans bring.

(Younger and younger, they all wear body-belts)

Thread in the eye,
the world grows smaller as the guts spill forth.

A splinter of desire, a "*Manuel*" trade.

(No one's ready for some football . . .)

And the laughing through the walls.

"The *shoes*, the *shoes*."

I'm tired of pathos.

This window looks out over all I own.

THE FUTURE OF THE NOMADS

The rain feeds exclusively on Paradise adult book store

it's sobbing for the lawyers

we came to watch from the gallery, planked
to arousal in our dresses
(insert flap A into slot B)

the invention of meteorology . . .

I wrote how the hundred martyrs
came blindly on all fours (into the bread kitchen)

how the magpie whistled

how he looked the other way . . .

The burning car is in a phylum of migratory attention-seekers

sew up the mouth and pray later

from this bed I can see a cloud of wrens
flying away from the solitary light fixture . . .

a hermit wads up
the electric bill

I can't wait any longer

my stitches keep exploding into bad ideas

MODELS DEMAND AND MUTATE

The trees are full of adjectives

a face like an elephant's
slowly falls apart in your binoculars

what about the zoning laws?

but they rub themselves all over the tree with those legs

a thousand to the bottle

one by one you might tie them to hooks

a loose sac unravels
in the stomach and the revival begins

Iodine

the perfect birth stone

Alas, it's the clock of the world

a candle burning

where the gears should be

AUTOMATIC THANK-YOU KISSES

Ordinary
men gather holding vote-sticks

but then came the end of that time

a whipsaw of radio congruencies

the battering of good manners

she caves

light frosts her bangs
while she shows off her unlocked story

the paparazzi remain sanguine

children who bite for the pleasure

and look at her salad

plosives and a nice tight
forehead wave crazily all over the outdoor mall

WORSHIP OF THE ASTONISHED

The menu looks fine

it's just there's a fly in that woman's sangria

a pair of crotchless
panties left under my windshield wiper

a baby differentiating
between self and a lime-green

stinkbug

They put one head right on top of the other

his eyes grew wild as two bird cages

the taste of something awful . . .

I know I woke up
and the sun was staring at me

Orange Juice

it's all about packaging

And the mockingbird knows something at 2 a.m.

The Riddler
Don Adams

Monks chanting in the alley

it wasn't at all *like yesterday*

she spoke as if from the top of a mountain

pubic hair on my cheek
and the crazy thing

unhooking its nozzle inside her

URN LIKE A WHORLED COCOON

(for John Woods, in memory)

He wore slippers
until they burned his feet

skin hardening

a bust like a fist inside him struggling to speak

in Nebraska the long grass blows north
and the sandhill cranes lean their long necks southward

it's conductivity

an allergy to simple grass

a tendency to drape clothes over exercise bikes

she got the call at ten "oh" seven

every child in her class began evaporating . . .

no good-bye kiss

not even a word

driving and driving over long bridges

LAKE GENESERATH

Orangutans

an oddity by any measure—

a seminal experience

breakthrough surrounded by strollers

a ring of ice blue in the wolf's eye . . .

phlebotomist takes a bite of salad

a fissure in the vein

the face you imagine contorts underneath your own

Poke, someone says in a child's voice . . .

way out in the mist of some lake an animal shoots itself

nobody speaks

his boat is one thing to love

the only thing moving for miles

OUR BLUEST SKIES

A liminal hum
in the leaves, an oriole's

disinterested
lodging

(a several-ounce barge)

You drive a second nail

sin tastes like that
it comes out of the shimmering blue like a chattering psalm

FIDELITY TO RAPTURE

Long morning past, still drinking

shock therapy on the beach, a haze of
gnats turning orbital . . .

it's this sand like an infestation

and the wind flipping a volleyball net . . .

O Harry Callahan

the silence surrounds you

already halfway to that deeper place

a gull runs along
the water's edge

rush of blood to the cerebral cortex

grass and twigs inside a jar for the walking stick

smell of a just-opened bag of pot

And childhood

the barking frog who used to live under my bed

those miraculous ribbons of smoke and the first cigarette . . .

Eleanor with her face turned
away from you

posing for the world and its manifold trees

I was just saying you never really
come to the end of this pier

LAKE CADILLAC

We were out under
The giant umbrellas

The long white sex of the moon shining—

Unblemished

The marble neck of Nefertiti—

On the bones of the last dinosaurs

The stars are an alignment of tear ducts

Allegorical triumvirate

A pinhole in the night for each wound

These comets
Of the new century—

Sentimental as liquid paper

Then an albino pigeon comes walking
Out of the bushes looking like Peter Lorre

I can't put a deterministic spin on it

The Heavenly Ham ® only partly defines the fork

Mars shining on the rim of the sky
Like a sinking diamond . . .

Stars reflect back to where she's softest

Where the water gets deepest

UNPOPULAR FILM

Said indulge

what kind of crap are you going to

it was a culvert
full of old mail

piles of garbage and graves rolling over in the wind

she put a single candle on a cupcake

as usual the woman was the screamer

and the man

the man

trembling at the prospect of pouring her tea!

there are nine of these carnivals

young girls find boys and they bruise them

the littlest saxophone
in Indiana

a keg in a claw-footed bathtub

helium doesn't make one's teeth turn green

and the character you like best is a literal monster

MIMICRY

A Viceroy lands on a Bose
Acoustic Wave . . .

Jonathan Richman and the Modern Lovers

a nodule sparks in a kingbird's brain

this music doesn't taste very good

and no one likes the hood ornament

standing erect

Limousine of the Antichrist

it's almost like his heart stains his trousers

the violent eruption of a migration

monarch bent and ringing against the roof of the mouth

angels are half human
half bird
what's that about?

Stones. Stones and the women who hoard them

or the unpopular lamprey eel

portals we leave when the love blows away

it's a whole new experience in headphones

the fish die from it

NERVOUS FILAMENTS

Slight successive modifications

you put on the blood
pressure cuff
a magnified period of grief kneeling in the Confessional

fly with his back legs rubbing together, praying

he sees a million of you!

I think everyone knows that famous still
from *Battleship Potemkin—*

my little friends

philosophy and remoras

the only fish that has a sucking disk on top of its head

did you just hear a baby?

a priest shouldn't have a tattoo of Darth Vader

there was sun shining all over the bed that beautiful morning

little silver penguins holding trays

may I suggest you seek the advice of a mental health professional

I put out some wine

microphones packed away neatly in a box
in the basement labeled

Shells of the Florida Panhandle

POSTCARD: CAPE MAY

A trance state in the particle
is par
for Massachusetts

the Red Sox

an expensive boat moored in the mud

ratio of lawns slept on
to the number of haircuts

certain other cars come roaring
out of the roundabouts

their wheels flying off

one man screams his prosthetic wit

they eat lobster with their bare hands . . .

tiny epics spill onto the docks there

the slut and his girlfriend

the family standing under a linden

(an abbreviation for pain)

a wedge of quartz suffers a panic attack

Charles Olson . . .

but night does come on slow

like giving up the piano for life

pathology of hungers

stairs made out of barn wood next to a luminous Coke machine

3. TO HOLD IN SUCH HIGH REGARD

"Whoever among you burnt the skiff knew
the flood would crowd us on this island"

John Woods, *The Valley of Minor Animals*

CONTRACT PLEASURE

1.

You are so made out of
Coke cans

less love-of-family than

bullet proof

the day the drought finally never came

an opulent
daydream of water

pears bursting

twelve-packs of Fresca in cans

The architects
left pieces of planning

all over the dam site—

an arm here

a saw horse with a man stabbed over it

a failure of mechanical law

2.

Then came the grafting of wretchedness

the Lilliputian shadow of last resorts
under the nose of an Airbus . . .

Oh such painful pleasures

High windows

Erasure of night

Francis Bacon knew how to make
religion out of such painted meat

the passion of ordinary love

How to Go Blind With It

(978-0-19-283580-2)

while Nietzsche just fell in a mud hole . . .

Forgetfulness . . .

not the bass thump of rap

but chanting coming over the dark skyline . . .

A terrified army of pleasure seekers

Rhinestones up the sides of your jeans

a stud in your tongue

WILDLIFE

Who needs Vermeer

all that standing in the filtered light with no job

a hundred days later

egg salad with pepper on white bread

a few humans standing around in the parking lot

fescue growing out of some painted pots

Victoria Secret was there, turning from a solid into a gas,
hovering over her salad

Next on News Center 8: Baltimore.

A place I visited.

I believe in words. One by one
they dismantle everything I have faith in

QUALITY IS PECULIAR TO CIVILIZED MAN

Yes, I took a polar siesta

one with a head like a pompom

good old pill-popper

and it is fragrance my friend we should worry to dust motes

Without aid
you can't tell exactly where
the hungry ant lives

plus an eyeball alone is just blind

It bleeds
and sings
whenever it's
lonely

a too rare steak
an uncomfortable ride

a little tank of gas for our journey along the naked thigh

(Land Ho!)

I implore you

the moon is cracking like a farm fresh egg

Don't be afraid of the eight ball

the reach-around fire escape

her love is just a bridge to cross

We know how to find what you need

DEMONSTRATES PROPER RELIANCE

Ill-fitting, rope
necklace

sweet as dessert the taste of smoke

the bird begins to think
like a man until it is identified

by a human being

a flag waving around in the woods
like an amplifier

a handful of human-growth hormone

(because mom put love
in your bowl of spinach)

I don't recall that kind of merry-go-round in my brain

a choir coming out
of the copy machine

She stands on a chair all night
with her head near the vent fan

Asleep on a bed of applause that grows slowly vague

you rise the next morning

to find it's only been snowing again

TACHYCARDIA

Natural and pure
coming right out

of the toaster

this sun on a recyclable plate

It's for you . . .

reminds you of the time you got the window seat

a gull flying outside
simply looked in at you

that was a good day . . .

and then the bag doesn't even
fit the vacuum cleaner

the tears
the tears

and they won't take the cups off your eyes . . .

I keep thinking of that ship

can it ever be extracted from inside the bottle
and if so

how does one stick it back in . . .

when she took off her shirt
I suddenly wanted to count to two

over and over again

how odd, she said, and searched the palm
of my hand for a lifeline . . .

no line of credit

it's called the human heart

MEDITATION: FARM POND

(Parma, Michigan)

There was a lack of transparency between

the clouds
and the bedrock

the cat's head slammed in the waffle iron
(so it looks like a waffle)

and the many clueless
species of butterflies mobbing the yellow laundry

geological lust sucked through the head

O migratory battalion
of stoic dandelions

the plain white house is a magnet for such invisible dossier

tell me what you think I was thinking
and I'll tell you rage is the outcome of

most reveries in Nature . . .

and the pike's huge head equaled a third of the trapped monk's
actual length

so what if we are sucked up the birth canal

accumulation of souls
each time the parents do it again

I don't want any more goose bumps, the hunchback cries in her sleep

she who is just like you

reptilian-plasma lodged in the brain between cold rudders

poor cowering girl

naked meat-eater

NOT A LANDSCAPE, NOT A TEASPOON

I know because
of the scratches

almost a perfect circle

Minnows sluggish
or heading to war

in the gray-green part of your eye—

a busted out headlight

Anomie ripples through the residential headquarters

I've come to this place

the luminous stage in an egg cup
made from the pumpkinseed's gill

I untie you

the smallest of lace currents

as the moon shows up howling like a train in the window

fills up the room
fills up his head

To hit her in the face is to
watch her head disappear

$6.90 for the reddest lipstick

a love nest in the suburbs where
she tries to please him most evenings

a pack of Winstons for mom

a tire iron gift-wrapped c/o Annapolis Steel . . .

Now it's raining on one half of your body

shadow under your armpit
our own proscenium arch . . .

The disembodied fingers—

they're only crayfish trying to leave home

And the brand new automatic garage door opener
slowly jerks the white door closed

for the very first time

NOT THERAPY

Sometimes you lock into some other's line of vision

let's call it today's "subject matter"

Some blessed
helmet of eyes

child left in the grocery store

the sister who got to fly to France

then there was that thing her father
said that hurt her . . .

puts a dent in your heart every time

sinuosity of the deformed psyche

It has wings

You drive a Honda

Mediocrity is simply a fact

you don't need therapy

it's not the fault of your priest

Pressed to murder for food

you might put your lyre
in a crate and run over it

Somebody invented glass
and they made a jail cell out of it

for you

with no door

The absolute opposite of zero
isn't poetry—

all these fresh graves

and not one animal praying

THEM

Magic conjoined,
complaining lilacs and the secret

fields,
a house made of tin

standing out loud in the center
of a narrative platform.

The rabbit appears.
She falls into a hole.

The rabbit doesn't get Trix.

He also planted hollyhocks,
disappointed two months later when they grew so . . .

hairy.

Cold northern pool
smooth as a mirror . . .

sex with no sound

birds all over the ceiling that are the words
he can't say

*

A magpie lands in a tree

It drops a stone in the water

Where are the stars now

TRAGEDY OF SPECIES

Stars fal-

ling

and then *Catch yourself*

that man has a pulmonary

way with his other

copacetic arrangement of plovers reading Wittgenstein

the murderer
used a sentence

she longed to own a minde of such durable compleasance

make love, not poetry

such methodical hunger

eat him up to his mountain

They all died

mourning

watch this reality filmstrip

HEART-SHAPED RECOVERY POEM

You'll come to once the
tube clears

memory of the way yellow taxis shine in the rain

tadpoles beside railroad tracks

the clamor of starlings

prime time for Oprah

and several full-moon lancings

And you know the balloon—

it opens

not to a face but an approximation of intelligent evil

Good Morning

It's the day after
the end of the world

and those aren't real horses

something peeled
down to speechless wood

duck after duck moving across the sealed windows

it happens even
while she's washing your hair . . .

TO HOLD IN SUCH HIGH REGARD

In terms that remain constant

it's something
they do

but you aren't some baseline in blue jeans

An autobiography's
an infestation . . .

like the men in her Muybridge study
a guitarist and a drummer
the gardener in his grandiosity . . .

"They are certainly no smarter than horses"

Pushing the linens back
we conceive a love

the
quality
of his leisure

it squeezes the hate right out of your finger

You might find one playing
in the dirt for example

sweating all over her instruments

A SMALL THING BUT MY OWN

(after a painting by Howard Hodgkin)

little arbitrary numbskull

the hand moves slowly into the public realm

we're sightless
from the mouth down

yellow where the label says yellow

art allows fresh captivity narratives

(the mad run through the mall
dashing paint onto unwilling shoppers)

but you and I

here's the slaughtering floor on a Sunday

birds free in the rafters

a rosary draped over your belly

the buzzard has a featherless head for a reason

our own Walk of Fame . . .

Beginning *before* we are named, that's what we do

but that's not why I'm running for Mayor

(looking for the perfect suicide note)

it's an artless apprenticeship for sure

too many beds at the registrar's

the laughter
the citronella

the deer out of nowhere watching through trees . . .

It's raining, I cried

paint flying everywhere

all over the frame,

the velvet, her nipples

a couple of early juncos

two snow birds

SYLVIA PLATH

1.

It's trenchant
if not quite verifiable

the metaphysical side of hand holding

the wrist bone connected to the

allegory of the unbendable spoon

professor, defendant . . .

Jeopardy is jejune

Rather a dervish
the eclipse of the animal senses

the silence of muscles moving under skin

combustible song

(in the mind of a Luna moth)

the braid of hair in your hand is thick as a rope

2.

And I don't care about *The Song of The Dead Man*

"the dead man buys batteries!"

"the dead man reads Milosz!"

the dead man's grave is a crop circle

enough with the dead man

3.

It's a marriage of privilege and a strong pair of thighs

the extraneous island of heaven

the silo of the dispossessed

they put the heads
in a glass case . . .

wild with vision from the belladonna

there must be a flood

silence like a tide rushing into the now open mouths

the old ways long gone for abusing the moon

MINOR SPRING FOG

I was still myself, a circle, wearing this bed

Offering what may not be

Fear breeding paycheck absence

Against hormones used for growth in normal children

Whose otherwise weather is brimming

A phrase you repeat

The mind knows fluently little of love

If you argue into wakefulness

Separation of your other self

THE HISTORIC DISTRICT

A dilapidation of channeling

things standing where you let them

pines in the wind shake out more pollen

(they're all sluts)

world I can trust because it isn't mine

the snow in the alley makes a little room—

this way you're no longer friendless

fully involved behind the shower curtain

(where there used to be a garden)

O gravity
O hot water

O delirious Sudafed buzz . . .

He kisses her hot, naked lips

O red rose she holds between her tits!

just think of the Midwest
as a giant Nativity Scene

(voice-echo in the porcelain cave)

I wouldn't say my thoughts race exactly

WILDERNESS

(Beaver Island)

It's not a matter of scale

(worthless imaginable)

a cup of tea for your doll

and cloud to ground lightning

he took it out behind his desk
and then he just looked at it

a fin growing out the back of his head . . .

Americana

Just do it

Essentially

I'm glad we are all grown up now—

(tall amongst the Michigan fruit trees)

glad our hands rest
on this same rocky island . . .

the smell of apples even inside the house

the window pane
the window pane

she used her checkered dress as a moonlight boat

looked out at the spruces
standing still under the Northern Lights

called them her Sentient Pines

COLUMBIA RIVER

the smell of the body

here at the river it disgusts us

or we can't talk past it

sweat and blood like so many simple fish . . .

the elephants go crazy in zoos
and believe me

we feel like them

the world is what you can see while breathing

I appreciate your not showering

words for how that feels

ripe like something buried and growing

NOTES

Some of the poems in *The Nervous Filaments* contain quotations, some slightly adapted, from Edmund Burke, Jean-Paul Sartre, Charles Darwin, Robert Hass, Fanny Howe, and Thomas Hobbes.

The movie *Junk Mail* got "Unpopular Film" started.

"I Am Never Going Back" references "Manuel" Ramirez, Detroit Lions, drafted 2007 . . .

"Born Late" owes something to Mott the Hoople, and, in particular, Overend Watts.

"Sylvia Plath": the collection of Plath materials at the Lilly Library in Bloomington, Indiana, includes a braid of the poet's hair, and they will bring it out, and you can pick it up.

"Minor Spring Fog" is a collage, assembled using pieces of text from Laynie Browne's *Daily Sonnets.*

I want to thank, for support and/or editorial insight, Louise Mathias, Dana Roeser, Paula Cisewski, John Gallaher, Nancy Botkin, Sally Ball, Charmi Karenen, and Ryan Murphy.

And thank you to Martha Rhodes. And Herb Scott—I miss you.

ACKNOWLEDGMENTS

Poems in *The Nervous Filaments* have appeared in the following journals, whose editors I here thank: *Barn Owl Review, Barrow Street, Court Green, Field, The Hat, Laurel Review, Natural Bridge, POOL, Quarterly West,* and *Zone 3*.

David Dodd Lee is the author of four other books of poems: *Abrupt Rural* (New Issues, 2004), *Arrow Pointing North* (Four Way Books, 2002), *Wilderness* (March Street Press, 2000), and *Downsides of Fish Culture* (New Issues, 1997). His fiction has appeared in *Controlled Burn, Crowd, Green Mountains Review,* and *Sou'wester.* Editor of the *SHADE* anthologies, he is also the publisher of Half Moon Bay chapbooks, which includes titles by Hugh Seidman & Franz Wright, and he was recently guest poetry editor for single issues of *The Laurel Review* and *Passages North.* Lee teaches at Indiana University South Bend.